I0653663

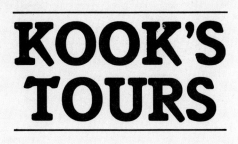

KOOK'S
TOURS

KOOK'S TOURS

prop. Stewart Cowley

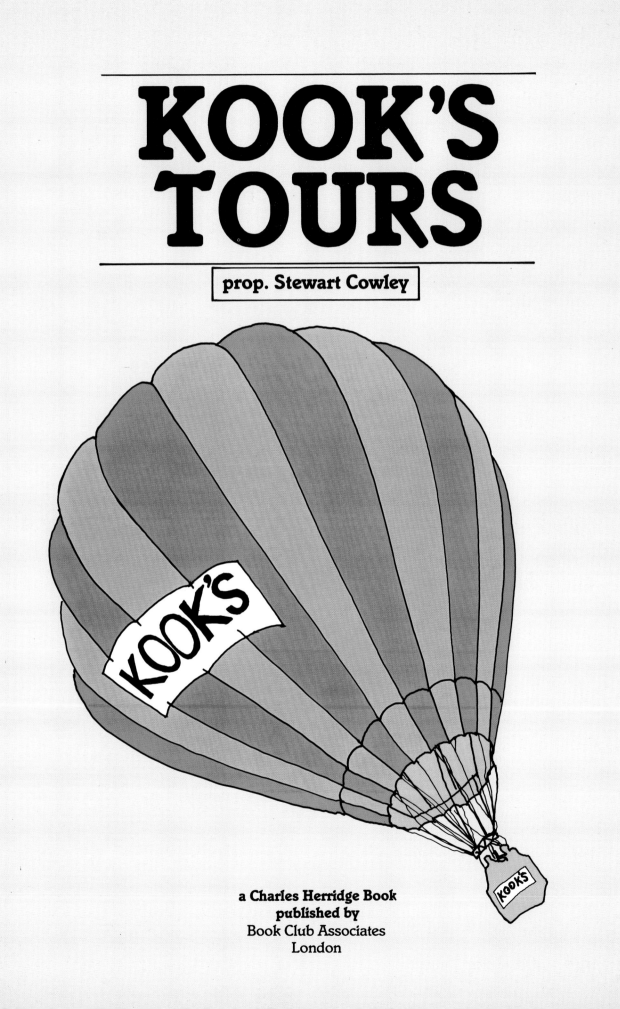

a Charles Herridge Book
published by
Book Club Associates
London

Copyright © by
Charles Herridge Limited 1983
This edition published in 1983 by
Book Club Associates
by arrangement with
Frederick Muller Limited
All rights reserved
Produced by Charles Herridge Limited
Tower House, Abbotsham, Devon
Printed in Italy by New Interlitho SpA, Milan

hi there Holidaymakers!

My name's Stewart Cowley (my analyst calls me Kook) and I'm your host here at Kook's Tours. When you turn over and start browsing through the lavishly printed, homemade pages of our superb catalogue you'll notice that our holidays are really different, and maybe you'll wonder why.

Well, here's how it all started. Last year I went on an Under 25s Singles Skiawayday. Boy was I bored. Climbing mountains and sliding back down on bits of wood was about as exciting as watching the TV test card. As I crouched in the hold of the plane on the way home I felt it would have been more exciting if I'd broken my legs. I was still brooding as I jumped from the hatchway on to the tarmac, and broke my legs. 'AAARGH!' I yelled. It was more exciting, alright – and so Kook's Tours was born. Here, at last, is a selection of holidays with *real* impact and *real* excitement. Here's where you meet the unexpected and test how you match up to it.

OK, so we had a bit of trouble last season, and I was suddenly called away to Brazil. But they've dropped all the charges now and here we are again, larger than life and offering so little for SO MUCH MORE!

Happy Landings, Funseekers!

Stewart Cowley.

Your No Fuel Surcharge Guarantee

Kook's Tours Guarantee that if there is **NO FUEL** there will be no **SURCHARGE**

Your Quality Guarantee

Kook's Tours Guarantee that if your **ACCOMMODATION** is not **OF THE HIGHEST QUALITY** you can always sleep somewhere else

Medical Note: Stewart Cowley is a paunchy, balding, 36-year-old divorcee who has to write stuff like this to get money.

Your Lives In Our Hands

From the moment you step into a Kook's Tours Office you won't be able to fault the quality of advice and personal service. This is mainly because there isn't any – to minimize wasteful overheads we refuse to employ any staff. The most up-to-date slot is provided and all you have to do is write down the holiday of your choice and insert it with a neatly folded bundle of money and your passport. As soon as you return home the unique excitement of 'Going with Kook's' begins. Will you get any tickets? Will they be for the holiday you chose? Will you ever see your passport again?

The answers to these and many other popular questions are probably, possibly, and no, in that order. The flourishing international trade in false identities enables Kook's to enjoy a financial stability that is the envy of all our competitors and it is you, the client, that benefits. We're not really sure why and that brings us back to our unique range of thrilling vacation ideas.

Our fabulous catalogue suits a wide range of tastes. Your personal particulars and requirements are fed into our powerful modern computer and, thanks to the magic of the micro-chip, are forgotten with breath-taking speed and efficiency. Our Complaints Department is second to none and we will start complaining to you as soon as your application has been received.

We know full well how tedious and time-consuming the making of travel arrangements can be so we leave everything to you. Once you have paid your money you can rely on us to use our incomparable knowledge and experience of the travel business to get as far away from you as possible.

GOING ON HOLIDAY
HINTS AND TIPS

Luggage
The word is derived from Lug: to drag or carry, and Gage: to assess or measure, and represents the quantity of chattels you consider to be worth transporting. As you are unlikely ever to see it again we recommend that you restrict your packing to household waste, garden debris and old mattresses or refrigerators. Wear all the clothing you think you may need during your holiday when you set off, and ask for a wheelchair. Considerable savings can be made by wearing the suitcase as well, but avoid sudden movements or loud noises on your arrival. This will prevent delays due to the need to revive the customs official who open you for inspection.

Documents
Keep all your identification documents in one place for peace of mind If you lose one you lose them all and can stop worrying about them. You will also become eligible for our New Identity Scheme. As part of our Rest In Peace Offer, deposit your Share and Bond Certificates, Savings Accounts, Property Deeds and Insurance Policies with us. Once you have signed our Deed of Trusteeship we will make sure you go away as rapidly and quietly as possible. Before travelling with us you should make sure that you have a valid Certificate of Release from your asylum.

Pets
To save time and trouble later, take only those that will not crease or wrinkle easily. Choose a versatile selection that will be suitable for both evenings and daytime, and can be packed quite tightly. The following are good examples: ants, pythons, dachshunds and amoebas.

Vaccinations

It is important to ensure that you have had all necessary inoculations unless you are prepared to spend six months in kennels on your return. If you are uncertain, refer to the checklist below:

Yellow Fever – Scarlet Fever – Blackheads – Blue Funk – Envy – Pneumonia – Old Monia – Halitosis – Hardpad – Spots.

Elderly travellers should check that they have been inoculated against Venerable Disease and a tuberculosis vaccination will make sure that you do not become a root vegetable.

Travel Sickness

Proprietory medicines are expensive and unnecessary. A litre of wet cement will steady the stomach equally well at a fraction of the cost. Do not exceed this amount if you wish to avoid excess weight charges. For long journeys it is worth considering having gimbals implanted. If sickness is unavoidable refrain from wan smiles; if your timing is out, the target area increases four-fold and this will not be appreciated by your fellow passengers. Alternatively, remain inside a dustbin liner for the duration of the journey.

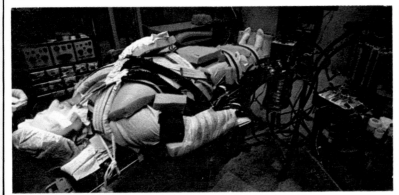

Travel and the Law

Before departure, familiarize yourself with local laws and customs. If you find that you have committed some inadvertent misdemeanor, swing one leg forward, placing the foot firmly on the ground. Shift your bodyweight forward from the other leg and allow the latter to swing forward one pace. Balance its weight by moving the opposing arm to the rear. Repeat this action with the opposite pair of limbs as swiftly as practicable and continue this sequence until out of trouble.

Money

Provided you are carrying small denomination used notes our agents will take care of this matter. An ice-pack will reduce swellings and minor contusions caused by selfishness. Remember, foreign money is very confusing and is best left to our experts.

Travel and Safety

Read carefully all safety instructions relevant to your mode of transport and familiarize yourself with exit and assembly points. As an added precaution, wear your Mae West fully inflated at all times but be careful not to puncture it when getting in or out of the car. Should an emergency occur, scream very, very loudly and run in extremely small circles. This will take your mind off things. Be prepared for accidents by carrying a large box of paper tissues as you will probably be expected to clean them up yourself.

Coping with Foreigners

Most of you will have encountered some foreigners in your daily lives and many of them seem really quite normal. In fact, it is often quite difficult to tell them from real people until you get close enought to detect their characteristic scent. Even then, although an oily skin is a sure give-away, modern toiletries can make positive identification almost impossible.

Silly Languages

Part of the fun of going abroad is observing foreign people in their natural habitat. The most striking thing is their obvious confidence and their reluctance to speak properly. Their habit of chattering in the gibberish known as 'foreign language' must be excused as they have not enjoyed the benefits of a proper upbringing in a civilized society. They can also be quite trying at times, but this is due to the sense of inferiority they feel in your presence. The fact that the more insistent you are in dealing with them, the more they jabber and wave their arms about, makes this very clear.

Foreign Muck

The question of what to eat will depend on the degree of risk you are prepared to accept. Obviously you will take as much proper food with you as space allows, but there will be times when necessity or a sense of adventure will lead you into eating local foods. By and large it is pretty filthy stuff so don't be afraid to insist that you are present in the kitchen to supervise the preparation of your food. They will certainly be grateful for your advice.

Don't worry unduly about local laws and customs as these are not meant to apply to you. But it is always possible that you may find yourself in a tricky situation when they are being a bit difficult. The secret of communicating with foreigners lies in using the minimum number of words spoken slowly, clearly and in a very loud voice. In particularly obstinate cases you may have to resort to adding -a, -o or -ee to the ends of words, e.g. The pedestriano justa ram-a-my radiatoree witha his head. In extreme cases you will have to resort to other measures (*see* Going On Holiday – Travel and the Law).

Useful Phrases

It's a traffic jam	C'est une confiture de circulation
Here we go	Oui bon bien alors on y va
It's curtains	Ce sont les rideaux
OK	OK
Better than a slap in the face with a wet fish	Mieux qu'un coup dans le visage avec un poisson mouillé
A lot of bull	Tora Tora Tora
Cheese and donkey sandwich	Sandwich de queso y burro

We have lost Keith	Abbiamo perso Keith
I think my neck's broken	Je crois que mon cou est... er... kaput
I love the French	Cochon
We adore Germany	Schweinhund
Please give generously	Baksheesh
I want to go home	Taxi!
OK, I'll talk	OK, je parle

Danger Sign Words

Achtung Spitfeuer	Here comes another British swine
Chute de Pierre	Falling executives
Foutez le camp	Leave my tent alone
Wally Wally	You next
Péage	Toll booth ahead
Mañana	Never
Hotel de Luxe	Towering inferno
Mayday Mayday	We are going down by the bows/stern
Pericoloso sporghersi	Gentlemen lift the seat
Dégustation de Vins	Poison, not to be taken internally

Swearwords

Thunder and Lightning!	
Name of a Dog!	Donner und Blitzen!
Big Jobs!	Nom d'un Chien!
Spherical Objects!	Merde!
	Cojones!

Some Difficult Words

	French	Spanish	Italian
Bar	Bar	Bar	Bar
Beer	Beer	Beer	Beer
Football	Football	Football	Football
Hotel	Hotel	Hotel	Hotel
Sex	Sex	Sex	Sex
TV	TV	TV	TV

Big Apple Climbing Holiday

- **HURTLE PAST VIPs**
- **PEER INTO SELECTED PENTHOUSE PADS**
- **HANG OUT IN ONE OF THE WORLD'S GREAT CITIES**

At first glance the sheer granite face soared into the luminous fog above without a single interruption to its glassy surface. The climber swayed with fatigue, his heart pounding and the perspiration beading his brow like small jewels. He glanced down just past his boot-tips as he ran his tongue over his cracked, parched lips. There were people down there as indistinguishable as ants scurrying about their obscure business unaware of the tense battle for survival taking place far above.

He was alone, truly alone. 'Oh God,' he thought, 'I'm alone, truly alone'. He knew he was right. Just a few pain-wracking yards stood between him and safety. 'A few yards,' he thought. 'A few pain-wracking yards and I'll be safe.' He was right again. Things were starting to go his way. He clenched his jaw hard and turned his muscular face back towards the unforgiving sheet of stone. Under his steely gaze the damp sheer surface began to yield its secrets to reveal a niche here, a small buttress there and above them, a narrow parapet. He was going to make it. 'I'm going to make it', he thought. The certainty lent new strength to his exhausted body, as his powerful fingers inched to-

Catering for every taste, Kook's offer nude, semi-nude and fully clothed climbs with attractive members of the opposite sex. Cranes, safety nets and expert instructors make you feel at home (subject to availabiilty).

48 Climbs to choose from

wards the first handhold, the muscles in his fingernails standing out like whipcords. Moments later he swung himself over the ornate parapet and staggered towards the elevator that would speed him down to the eleventh floor snack bar.

Crumbling Ledges

Neglected since the Wall Street Crash, the sport of urban mountaineering is enjoying a long overdue revival, and Kook's Tours now offer you the chance to discover for yourself the thrills and excitement that once sent scores of bored and out of condition businessmen scampering to the ledges and cornices of New York's spectacular architecture.

Unique Views

Peering into exclusive penthouses, abseiling past some of the highest paid executives in the world or traversing the difficult neon tangle of Times Square, you will see New York as few have. All climbs are carefully selected and graded to suit every level of experience from the easy but educational Brooklyn Bridge to that old favourite The Empire State Building, the Chrysler Building or the sheer and daunting façade of the United Nations block.

King Kong

In the words of one of the greatest of the old-time urban mountaineers, Mr. K. Kong, 'Whoo urgh unnh whoo whoo!'

EXPERT INSTRUCTORS
and luxury facilities

Inexperience need be no impediment to your full enjoyment of a climbing holiday; many of our expert instructors have almost none themselves. Although you may bring your own equipment if you prefer, we can supply everything you are likely to need; our office has piles of thick string (some of it very strong indeed), crampons, pitons, neurons, ganglions, tampons and things like miniature pick-axes.

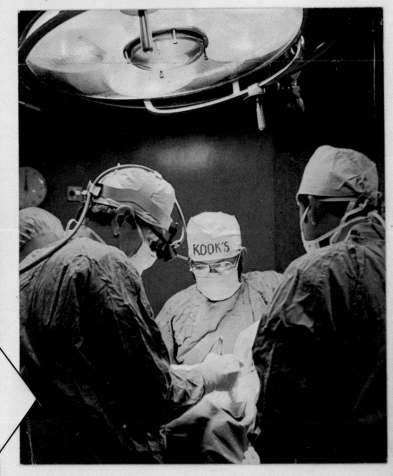

A full back-up staff stands by for an hour or two every day to help you make the most of your experience. Here they are shown making up one of the packed lunches that are so vital to the success of any major expedition.

Wildlife Safari

HUNT DEADLY WORMS
with our local experts

SEE NATURE IN THE RAW—Nudist safaris

EAT REAL PEOPLE

RUN FROM DANGER

See nature in a way you never dreamed was possible or even desirable. Become a part of a spectacular food chain in some of the world's greatest zoos without bars in a way which is fun for you, fun for your family and fun for lots of predators.

In these times of the global village it seems hard to imagine those far-off days when half the known world was unknown. Now, with a Kook's tour Super Safari you can plunge through trackless jungles just like those intrepid explorers of yesteryear.

Real Leeches!

Find out for yourself what a lion's breath smells like, pluck real leeches from your bronzed flesh, run away from dangerous things! As part of our deluxe package, we undertake to parachute you and your family deep into the unmapped wilderness of your choice where simply everything is red in tooth and claw.

Baggy Shorts

While you are waiting for our specially selected native guides to arrive you can change into the solar topees and baggy shorts supplied by courtesy of Kook's Tours. But the fun doesn't end there. As soon as you are ready, our guides will lead you deep into the impenetrable jungle, and once you have lost your bearings, will drop your baggage with incomprehensible cries and melt into the leafy gloom.

Relish the thrill of discovery as you study your surroundings and realize just how many dangers there are. Gasp with horror at your predicament, sigh with relief as our cheery guides spring out of their hiding places, gasp with yet more horror as you realize that they're not our native guides after all! Learn at first hand all about the cooking and serving of unusual and very personal local delicacies.

All too soon the great adventure will

from **£297**

Packed lunches will be provided for each excursion and will consist of flavoursome local delicacies. Those enjoying our deluxe Safari will have ample opportunity to offer themselves as packed lunches to the loca fauna.

be over, but think of the tales of discovery and excitement you will have to tell your envious friends on your return. Become the centre of attention at any social function with your suntanned body ravaged by all manner of strange and exotic diseases, puffy with the bites of a thousand Tsetse Flies, eyes fixed on uncharted horizons.

Elephant Droppings

For those with a limited budget, Kook's Tours can offer all the atmosphere and excitement of a safari in the comfort of your own home. With the help of a local florist, a box of gaily chirping crickets and a few buckets of elephant droppings, our experienced staff can transform your home into an African jungle.

Learn to track the secretive earthworm to its subterranean lair, swelter in the steamy hell of a dozen convectors heaters as you listen apprehensively to the blood-curdling squeaks of mice padding round the dying embers of your backboiler.

Whichever package you choose, a Kook's tour Wildlife Safari offers you a truly once-in-a-lifetime experience you are unlikely to forget for days.

Free Medical Insurance

Executive Credit Card Spree

- **Write Big Numbers**

- **Bark into Phones**

- **Go In Planes**

- **Eat International Dog's Dinners**

Sweet Smell of Success

Have you ever envied the life of the top executive as he jets from meeting to meeting, wines and dines in the highest style and talks into two telephones at once? Why not try it for yourself on our Executive Credit Card Spree? **Be a real tycoon** for seven glorious days of frantic rushing about.

By paying a substantial lump sum into our special credit account you can join our exclusive Executive Club for a week. In return you will receive an eyecatching golf credit card, a tiny hand-tooled crocodile briefcase and a personalized computer link to our international Monopoly game.

Buy and sell prime international locations, build office blocks, get out of jail free!

Each briefcase comes to you packed with Important Documents and sets of thrilling Company Accounts. Browse through them as you hurtle through the darkness in a chauffeured limousine to catch the night flight to Zurich. Once aboard, intrigue your fellow first-class passengers with your complimentary In-Flight Kit. This includes multi-million pound Profit and Loss Accounts, a gold-plated and absolutely minute calculator and matching gold pen with rubberized safety tip for tapping pensively against the front teeth (not supplied). The hostess will interrupt you at least once during the flight with urgent messages via the aircraft's ground link. And a current copy of the Times crossword with the answers pencilled in is provided for you to dash off during inflight cocktails.

Important Meetings
At the other end a uniformed receptionist will whisk you through customs and into another limousine. A realistic dummy car telephone is provided for use during traffic jams. Rush into important meetings, give firm pep-talks and rush out again.

No previous business experience necessary!

A list of business conferences and shareholder's meetings taking place at each destination will allow you to put our Groomed for Power Pre-Holiday Seminar into practice. Take your place on the rostrum with international Captains of Industry with confidence. Your air of stern authority will discourage anyone from asking who on earth you are. For real impact, wander out in the middle of the Chairman's Address.

A KOOKS Bigtimer HOLIDAY

Hot Dinners

A list of the world's most expensive wines is furnished to enable you to order in a loud voice when entertaining in exclusive restaurants. Our local representative 'clients' are well trained in awe-inspired deference and will hang on your every word. Discuss billion dollar deals in public. Make disparaging remarks about leading financiers. Pull fistfuls of the wrong currency from your pocket when buying drinks in nightclubs.

Wherever you are, our agents will page you, bring telephones, deliver telexes every fifteen minutes. A photofile of local business figures enables you to send over bottles of wine whenever you see them in restaurants or clubs. Acknowledge their puzzled but friendly waves with warm condescension, and pat them on the back as you leave.

Discover the pleasure of prompt service and admiring glances. Excite envy. Learn to smile with your mind obviously elsewhere and to switch instantly from lively bonhomie to crisp efficiency with the arrival of yet another telephone.

Your mother's heart will burst with pride when you send her one of our Jumbo Personalized Postcards. Be the son she always wanted!

CREDICARD

free
DIGITAL AFTERSHAVE
CLOCK RADIO
CALCULATOR
ALARM

Espionage Excursion

The single streetlamp does no more than deepen the shadows in the silent backstreet as you tug the brim of the fedora lower and turn up the collar of your grubby trenchcoat. Flicking the cigarette end away in a fiery arc you walk quietly towards the little alley that runs behind the embassy building. A few steps and you are at the back door. A quick glance tells you that it is a simple three tumbler cylinder lock, and as soon as the alarm wires are cut, you are inside and moving swiftly and soundlessly up the stairs to the file room. A sudden movement and the security guard is out of the way while you extract the vital file and run through a roll of 16mm film. Then it's out the way you came in, with a pocketful of secrets and the knowledge that the Western World is safe once more.

Meet Your Mata Hari

Spies come in all shapes and sizes and there is no reason why yours wouldn't fit the bill as well. If you

long to slink about in places where you are not supposed to be and stuff messages into hollow trees, then a Kook's Tours Espionage Excursion is just what you want. Our induction seminar will teach you all about cryptography, electronic surveillance and silent sidling about in thirty-nine easy to follow steps.

A Career in the Circus

Once you have grasped the rudiments of furtive darting into doorways and pushing people out of fast trains you are ready for a fun fortnight sticking your nose into other people's business and biting **free cyanide capsules**. If you are furtive enough you could find yourself working with legendary dwarfs like Smiley, Happy, Grumpy, Dopey or Sneezy. They will be your contacts and will brief you on your missions.

Your spy equipment will be

Get a FREE Radio-Razor, and communicate with your Spymaster with our up-to-date telepathic headwear.

could be done by someone else in the comfort of a romantic embassy basement. Your spying holiday will certainly not lack variety with electronic bugs to plant, atomic plants to bug and frontier post barriers to smash through. Why lie around on sun-soaked beaches when you could be dodging huge foreign agents on the Orient Express or liquidating interesting strangers? Whether spying in the interests of national security or simply to discover the secret of hush-hush tonic waters remember that Kook's word is your Bond.

Make attractive new friends in your search for top secret installations, and end your mission in the arms of a handsome U-boat captain.

issued FREE from the department store and will include a code book for international calls, gumshoes for sticky situations, an exploding briefcase and a false nose. These should all be eaten if you fall into enemy hands. If you are very seriously captured you should also eat yourself beginning at the opposite end to your teeth.

Shot From Torpedo Tubes

Imagine the thrill of parachuting into pine forests or being shot from a submarine's torpedo tube onto an isolated beach with a briefcase full of false passports and chocolates. Apart from filming important government officials and scientists in compromising positions there is plenty of opportunity, if you hold a current driving licence, for driving like a maniac with diplomatic immunity and snapping your fingers at danger (car not included).

If you enjoy the company of others the snapping of your fingers

Kulture Kruises

- **DRAW SEVERAL THINGS**

- **MAKE VALID STATEMENTS**

- **WEAR SANDALS**

Inside every human being lies a great artist struggling to escape, and only the force of circumstances prevents everybody from making their own valuable contribution to our cultural heritage. As we all know, producing masterpieces of perception and sensitivity takes quite a lot of time, and evenings and weekends are often just not enough.

Some people try to give their creative urges elbow room by attending art and craft centres, but knitted egg-cosies and terracotta ashtrays just aren't in the big league artwise.

As Many Masterpieces As You Can Paint!

On a Kook's Kulture Kruise the whole family has the chance to

create really significant masterpieces in two uninterrupted weeks of furious creativity. All you have to do is synthesize the implicit truths of spatial and chromatic harmonies, redefine your perception of **environmental plasticity** through the symbolistic interrelationship of colour, form and texture, grow little pointed beards and **smoke exotic substances**.

Don't worry if you haven't done internationally recognized masterpieces before; our beginner's course is designed specially for you. Expert instructors will show you how to pile bricks into shapes worth thousands of pounds and the whole family can join in. While your children are out collecting creatively witty *objets trouvés* on the local dump, you can have a go at painting the Sistine Chapel by numbers in one of our breathtaking derelict warehouses.

Great art is nearly always ridiculed by contemporary society, and the greater the art, the more intense the

Skilled tutor Chuck Rembrandt teaches you every trick in the book . . .
. . . even how to save time and paint by using a roller (choose from Goya or Hockney Styles).

BOOK NOW for Plasticene Welding and Concretism.

Edie O'Baxter puts finishing touches to her biggest-ever corned beef work. Husband Donald is snapped below with his prize-winning Palladian Palazzo, exhibited at '82 Benidorm Salon till the tide came in.

ridicule. We therefore have every reason to believe that our Kulture Kruises consistently produce works of a standard as high, or higher, than anything ever produced before. Many of our first-time clients choose to enroll in our Naive Art course, and if you have any doubts as to your ability to paint, then this is the one for you. The enrolmemt fee is £12,473 and if you are prepared to pay this you will really be naive.

Nudes Galore

Our courses cover the whole spectrum of modern and traditional art. Throw paint-covered nudes at huge canvases, throw elderly ladies at watercolours of the village church, draw moustaches on famous portraits and be a Surrealist. Draw impressions and be an Impressionist, draw fast trains and be an Expressionist, draw square things and be a Cubist, draw round things and be a Cyclist.

If you find the broad expanse of virgin canvas or the block of marble too inhibiting and cannot bring yourself to even touch it . . . fear not. Just proclaim that it stands as a valid statement of your purity of vision or your respect for the inalienable right of things to remain unviolated. Remember always that 99% of being an artist is acting like one. If you are vehement enough and use enough complex but meaningless phrases, no-one will feel able to con-

tradict you. If they do, you can always resort to the supercilious smile taught in our Posturing Class.

On the last day of your holiday we have arranged for a number of prominent critics to visit your exhibition, clap their hands in gleeful appreciation and endorse your application for an Arts Council grant.

STOP PRESS: Rubens and Botticelli Fleshtravaganza Fully Booked.

Work-a-Way Job Jaunts

Every year more and more people take the big step of being thrown out of their jobs, only to discover that they have simply exchanged one tedious routine for another. Before long the novelty has worn off and it's time to start thinking about holidays.

For the unemployed the choice is limited. What's the point in paying good money just to lounge around eating, drinking, sleeping and wondering what to do next? Hardly a change of routine is it? Look no further, for Kook's Tours has the answer . . . Work-a-Way Job Jaunts.

Real Wages

A few spare pennies deposited in our special fund each week and a real job for two fun-packed weeks could be yours. The only extras to pay for are board, lodging and your travel arrangements. All your wages will be paid to us, so you can forget about Income Tax and

enjoy the dignity of labour

without a care in the world.

Work up a real sweat, rediscover the thrill of callouses and compacted vertebrae. Savour the old-world

tradition of mindless, repetitive labour and the exhilarating surge of dumb frustration at your exploitation. Forget books and crossword puzzles and let your mind stagnate like real workers. All our jaunts are

guaranteed labour-intensive

and you can choose from a wide range of exotic workplaces.

Chain Gangs

How about an unforgettable trip to the unspoilt United States and the historic panoramas of the Mississipi delta? Beat yo' feet in da Mississipi mud and sing about boll weevils as you scamper happily from bush to bush picking cotton in the time-honoured way. Join thousands of migrant workers in the sun-kissed fruit fields of California or Florida, where you can pick oranges for up to 14 hours! When the day's toil is over the many informal ethnic restaurants offer the chance for a little part-time dishwashing before you topple contentedly into your genuine handcrafted bunk.

For the more ambitious would-be worker we can offer our Supasweat

Specials. Wallow in work ethic in the famous salt-mines of colourful Siberia or the sweatshops of exotic Taiwan. Work your fingers to the bone in appalling conditions among friendly Lascars on the 'rusty tubs' of maritime folklore. Or you can claw the yellow ore from the earth thousands of feet below the South African goldfields and be really fulfilled.

For a first-rate family work-in nearer home, why not try one of our

popular work camps? Thanks to the donations of our many clients we have purchased several old wartime airfields and can offer you **hours of futile labour.**

Spend the first happy week digging trenches and holes in reinforced concrete runways under the expert supervision of our ex-Ministry staff. Sunday afternoon is spent cleaning tools before the second week of filling in and making good. Do not forget a visit to our camp shop to stock up with duty-free embrocation and mouth-watering rubbing alcohol.

Redundant office workers can spend hours piecing together documents from our modern paper shredders and making triplicate copies of the local telephone directories in longhand. Recapture those golden days of repressed hysteria and physical stress in superbly inadequate conditions with Kook's.

Sir Jasper Medieval Joustabout

A hush falls on the motley crowd as the massive, gaily caparisoned chargers snort and paw the ground. The sun glints on corselet and helm, plumes flutter in the light summer breeze. A handkerchief drops and with a rattle of harness, the great steeds thunder towards each other. The ground shudders, colours dance and shimmer as the heavy lances are levelled. There is a splintering crash as the shock of impact is echoed in the roar of the crowd and a figure sprawls in the dust. The victor raises his visor and turns to the royal stand. The princess's hand is his.

Come back with us to those glorious days of yore when chivalry was in full flower. Take your place at our hand-tooled Round Table in the Sir Jasper Medieval Joustabout and **be a knight for more than just a day**. Walk around in a metal suit saying authentic medieval words like 'knave' and 'varlet' and smiting things with a huge antique-style spiky mallet.

Fair Maidens and Swarthy Saracens

Have a go at our Select-a-Quest Lucky Dip and win a lady's favour. Fight small dragons (well, lizards actually). Climb up ladies' pigtails or do battle with Unknown Knights. For the latter, clients can choose from three different sizes: standard, small or tiny. Cleave Saracens from gullet to gizzard with real, hand-honed swords on the field of honour. A separate area is set aside for the inexperienced where they can battle to the death with pillows or raspberry canes.

There are games, contests and activities to suit every taste. Go surfing with real serfs! Throw down gauntlets! And don't miss our special seminars on brandishing with halberds, pikes and the deadly portcullis. Tilt at the quintain, gallop at the tilt, disguise fair nature with hard favoured rage! For those who lack riding experience we can supply small wooden horses you push along with your feet.

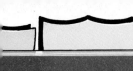

When you're not rescuing maidens or sacking castles, take time off to wander the picturesque streets of our quaint medieval village. You can pop into the barbershop for a quick shave and a pound of leeches, or visit our middle age tailor. He will be happy to kit you out with suits of mail, tabards of silk and coats of arms. Holiday Hint: middle age tradesmen just love to haggle, so don't spoil their fun!

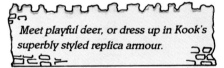

Meet playful deer, or dress up in Kook's superbly styled replica armour.

Foaming Firkins

After a hard day's questing what could be better than a relaxing wassail with your fellow knights. Quaff horns of ale, **eat whole boars** with your bare hands (Kosher feasts by special arrangement) and throw bones at dogs. Laugh very loudly and wipe your greasy fingers on your beard (supplied free to unaccompanied ladies). For those with a careful eye on their waistlines we provide a no-calorie Dungeon Dinner in our Iron Maiden Snackerette.

When you have wined and dined your fill, dance the night away to the insistent throb of sackbut and dulcimer or play for a king's ransom in the Camelot Casino. Then it's off to the tower for a good knight's rest before tomorrow's packed programmed of pillaging, hawking and spitting.

Here it is! The ultimate whirlwind tour for hard-pressed culture vultures. Why spend precious weeks every year touring small bits of foreign parts?

See the Whole World in One Weekend.

No more hanging about in strange hotels trying to get your cleaning back. No more tramping the streets looking for things to point your camera at. No more wandering for hours round echoing art galleries and museums. Best of all, no more roaming from weird little restaurant to weird little restaurant in search of a decent hamburger.

- **See every proper country in the world in air-conditioned comfort in the time it takes to order dinner in a Paris bistro.**

- **Spend 96 hours chasing your luggage in trains and boats and planes while absorbing the cultural, social and political heritage of the entire world.**

- **Amaze your friends and impress your workmates with your global knowledge and experience.**

As soon as our wide-bodied jet takes off for breakfast in Paris the first film show begins. See the Tuileries, the Louvre, the Eiffel Tower and hear tapes of accordions and people speaking real French. Wine labels and paté wrappers are issued to stick into your souvenir folders.

At Orly airport the snack bar is right next to the duty free shops, so you can grab a Pierre Cardin tie before boarding for lunch in Frankfurt airport. Postcards of the Reichsmuseum and the Red Light District as well as pieces of sauerkraut can be stuck in your folders en route for Rome.

Cobras and Betel Nuts

Look down on the Coliseum as the aircraft turns north to Budapest and admire a spectacular view of the Forum. Hear tapes of Ferraris as we issue empty Chianti bottles made into tablelamps by real Sicilian peasants. Dinner over Hungary and

The cabin of our jetliner soon develops a pleasantly informal atmosphere, especially when the toilets get blocked up.

Youthful Captain Deacon has already piloted eight Kook's global tours at the age of only 23.

Roumania to the strains of gipsy violins . . . then time for a little nap before landing in Baghdad for the second day's breakfast. A quick bus trip to the Gulf and a packet of romantic Arabian sand. Then off to Bombay for a betel nut and chapati sandwich. Spend an entertaining hour or two trying to get your stuffed cobra into your folder before landing in Djakarta for a photosession with the Kook's Tours headhunters.

A KOOKS
Jetlagger
HOLIDAY

Aloha Manila

Ah . . . the mysterious East. How inscrutable it looks from 30,000 feet. Savour our soy-sauce-flavoured burgers and laugh at chopsticks as the firecrackers explode in the gangway to the sound of a temple chant. To while away the Pacific crossing our versatile hostesses will do Australian accents while issuing tasteful kangeroo-skin beercan holders and traditional platypus hot water bottle covers.

Then scamper off for an hour in the surf at Monterey while we refuel for the exciting trip to Rio de Janeiro. As you board, collect your package of Sombrero, Sioux arrowhead, Navajo silver belt buckle and bottle of Niagara water containing a Canadian maple leaf.

Lounge in your FREE LLAMA HAIR BANLON MIXTURE BEDSOCKS as the train speeds across the Pampas for a boat trip across the Amazon before the flight to Africa. Gaily decorated aerosol cans of lion scent and the vibrant sound of hornbills in full stereo bring to life the rich variety of wildlife photographs. As we zig-zag over as many African states as possible you can mount your genuine replica elephant ears in your folders and look forward to the taxi ride home.

Kook's eye view of Trafalgar Square, London, England – a sample of the vibrant vistas we offer you.

Funseekers wanting to make unscheduled stopovers are catered for too. Our vivacious hostesses will open the door for you just anywhere! (Parachutes payable cash in advance.)

● **FREE SOUVENIRS**
● **FREE DEODORANTS**
● **FREE BENZEDRINE**

Tired but radiantly happy, funseekers pass through the gaily-decorated customs hall at Kook's International Airport on arrival home.

Krazy Kult Kapers

- **Chant Round The Clock**
- **Wear Colourful Robes**
- **Meet Voodoo Chickens**
- **Burn FREE Incense**

In these multi-denominational days of fragmented faiths and diverse devotions, the spirit is often willing but the flesh is confused. Religious conformity is decidedly outmoded in today's world . . . but what are the fashionable alternatives?

Should one seek admission to a non-conformist faction within an orthodox faith, the orthodox faction within non-conformist one or something else entirely, like singing to trees? From Flat Earth to Polytheism the spectrum of choice is mind-boggling. Indeed, Mind-Boggling may itself be a valid form of worship.

Let Kook's Tours help by offering you the chance to try a selection of some of the latest ideas. Consult our theosophical experts for the ones best suited to you. Booking with us admits you to the sect of your choice as a Full Member and each holiday comes with a booklet of key phrases and chants and the appropriate raiment tailored to your very own personal body.

Is Voodoo for You?

For those long summer breaks how about one of our Sun Worshipper getaways? Run round sacrificial stones on sun-splashed beaches or cavort naked in quaint Polynesian settlements. If it's nightlife you're interested in, how about a Voodoo Vacation? Learn the inside facts on chickens and eye-rolling. Dance yourself into hysteria to insistent pounding rhythms.

Among the newer Nature-orientated faiths we can offer a week among the Mermons who believe that the sea is the birthplace of all life and that dolphins are our true custodians. Spend a week at a first class aquarium where you will be fitted with a superb rubberized dolphin suit and taught to speak in staccato squeaks while leaping twenty feet into the air to catch herrings. **Learn to use a blowhole!**

Our family package will fit your

Wear Really Great Mystic Robes

Learn to be a Real Fanatic

Play Reincarnation Roulette

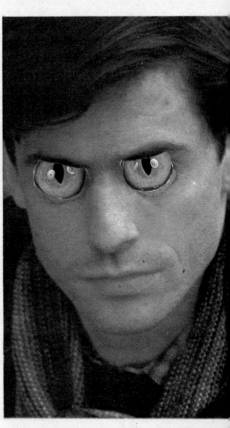

group into a whale if you prefer something more biblical.

Meet Real Crazies!

A more conservative holiday manages to combine religious fervour with low, low prices in that ever popular mystical resort . . . India. On our **Fakir Funweek** you can spend fourteen days cross-legged with your arms in the air without moving, eating or sleeping. We even offer a Stay-at-Home deal for minimum cost enlightenment that comes with free incense, shrill music and cobras.

For the younger holidaymaker, how about a week of **Electro-Existentialism** which teaches that true purity of thought and being can only be found in the micro-chip? Leading computer experts will link your brain to some of the world's most advanced terminals. Save the Earth from the forces of evil through positive thinking. The highest score at the end of the week gives the winner a FREE circuit test and service.

Spend a week in the city of your choice with the Doomsday Merchants. We supply a quality sandwich board and an ample supply of ashes. Moan lugubriously at passers-by from all walks of life and tear your hair out in handfuls. With our deluxe version you can listen to the crazed rantings of a top meglomaniac while performing a wide range of demeaning tasks. Your powerful FREE cyanide capsule comes with the compliments of Kook's Tours. May the Force be with you!

Bierkeller Beano

Beer, Beer, glorious beer . . . as much as you can drink and more. Fourteen days of non-stop beer swilling and the more you drink the cheaper the cost of the holiday. Although the cost of our bumper Bierkeller Beano may seem high in the cold light of morning, it can work out almost free if you drink solidly for 24 hours a day.

We have made special arrangements with **well over 100 breweries** across the length and breadth of Europe for you to be their guests in a packed programme of visits and tastings for **two wonderful weeks you will never remember.** Our luxury coach with its white-tiled interior will speed you from brewery to brewery in comfort. Regular stops are made for you to stretch those parts other Tour Operators can't reach while we top up with fuel and hose down the cabin.
GET DRUNK IN DORTMUND, WRETCHED IN WIESBADEN, VOMIT IN VIENNA. At each visit you will be met by the colourful chief brewer who will explain the various recipes and techniques used, while you are being connected to the storage vats. Then it's taps on . . . and the noble amber fluid is injected

under pressure to make sure each passenger gets his fair share.

As soon as everyone is full, our assistants disconnect you and roll you round the brewery for the brief inspection of the bottling plants and picturesque dispatch bays. Then back onto the bus and into the hammocks for a snack of mouthwatering dry crackers to create enough of an airspace to enjoy our selection of bottled beers from the travelling bar.

All The Beer In The World . . .
Learn not to care what the differences are between bitter, stout, lager, pilsner, porter, malts and ales. Learn the secret of the newt . . . become entirely spherical. A supply of international brews is carried to

allow you to make comparisons. For those of a more philosophical or spiritual turn of mind there is ample opportunity for quiet meditation or violent self-expression in the small cubicle at the rear of the bus.

. . . And Food Too!
In view of the large number of breweries to be visited, the itinerary makes no provision for any other stop, so a good supply of wurst and aspirin is carried on the bus for anyone feeling the need for solid refreshment. Our helpful and understanding staff will be happy to insert sausages into anyone unable to coordinate their limbs, according to a previously agreed schedule. An experienced tailor is at hand to let out

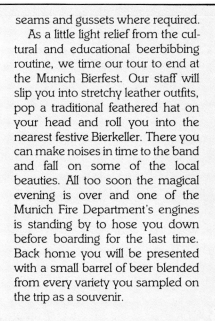

seams and gussets where required.

As a little light relief from the cultural and educational beerbibbing routine, we time our tour to end at the Munich Bierfest. Our staff will slip you into stretchy leather outfits, pop a traditional feathered hat on your head and roll you into the nearest festive Bierkeller. There you can make noises in time to the band and fall on some of the local beauties. All too soon the magical evening is over and one of the Munich Fire Department's engines is standing by to hose you down before boarding for the last time. Back home you will be presented with a small barrel of beer blended from every variety you sampled on the trip as a souvenir.

Self-Katering Survival Special

Being a rugged explorer is not an easy business these days. It is very expensive getting an expedition mounted and there are not nearly enough generous research foundations to go round. Besides, you would be competing with professionals with science degrees and huge beards. The cheap alternative, of course, is to join the army, but unfortunately, few services accept families and fewer still will accept anyone for just two weeks.

But before you resign yourself to foregoing the delights of hardship and deprivation in bleak and unmapped places, take a look at a new, low-budget package put together by our Family Holiday Department . . . the Self-Katering Survival Special.

God Forsaken Places

For next to nothing you can choose a destination from our God Forsaken Places file. We will then abandon you and your family there and as soon as your cheque has cleared, completely forget all about you. Learn self-reliance and toughness . . . invent new ways of preparing and serving close relatives under difficult conditions. Become a REAL MAN! Your wife and family can also become REAL MEN. And why not take your pets as well? It's a lot easier than having to carry your food supplies.

Sheer Hell

At the cheaper end of the scale, Dartmoor has proved a consistent favourite. Many of our clients have been so satisfied with this delightful venue that they have never returned home. Wander around in freezing fog and learn to live off the land. Chewing the lichen off rocks develops powerful and attractive cheek muscles for that really manly smile. Or you can enjoy those alfresco shopping expeditions when you hurtle out of the mist with bloodcurdling screeches to fall upon unsuspecting hikers.

Survival Hint: Boots and anoraks should be boiled over a low heat for at least thirty minutes to extract the full flavour.

Abroad

For a real getaway vacation why not choose the Swiss Alps? Imagine the rugged pleasure of waking on an icy ledge, shaving with shards of ice and rolling around naked in the snow for that fresh-all-over tingle. Spend hours hanging from ropes on vertical faces and learn to start fires by rubbing things *really* fast. And don't miss the avalanches of melting snow!

More expensive but still excellent value is our **Amazon Adventure.** While you collect fat beetles for picnic lunches, your children can enjoy wrestling the giant crocodile or friendly anaconda.

Shed those excess pounds instantly by falling into the piranha-

Enjoy a lipsmacking lunch of hot fresh rabbit, full of natural goodness . . . or let your kiddies get to know kind-hearted old Mrs Rhinoceros and her playful lamb.

A KOOKS Brutalizer HOLIDAY

infested water of this King of Rivers!

This may be your last chance to explore a vanishing wilderness. You can make contact with vanishing tribal societies. Turn your back on the tent for a few minutes and your possessions will have vanished as well. Other tribes are less timid and will take great delight in showing you the wonders of their country, carrying you and your family uncomplainingly for miles into the majestic rain forests slung from stout, springy poles. Once at their camp they wil almost certainly insist on having you for lunch.

Imagine how surprised your friends will be when you find your way back through cruel and inhospitable terrain with only a toothbrush and a woolly hat between you and a slow death. Imagine how surprised we will be too!!!

EXTRA WEEK FREE
IF YOU SURVIVE THE FIRST TWO

Why not try one of our Hang On To Your Breakfast Breaks, crammed with action-packed contests. For the less active, waiter service is available – with a smile.

Savour the flavour of giant roast hamster.

Feminist Festival

Calling all pretty, young mothers-of-two housewives! Here is your chance to step into the vanguard of the feminine revolution. Drop your pots and pans, abandon your whiter than white laundry, leave your darling husband's dinner in the oven and book a ticket to the Kook's Tours Feminist Festival.

Remember, you may think you enjoy pottering around the house while your man slaves his way through the daily, interminable grind. You may believe that looking after the children is all the fulfilment you need. You may even consider that meeting the demanding requirements of running a family home, budgeting and organizing the complex logistics of domestic life is as challenging as any commercial enterprise. But you are WRONG! You are, in fact, a traitor to your sex!

Blazing Panties

Learn to be shrill! Discover the excitement of burning underwear in the company of some of the world's leading exponents of the art. Get trapped in conversation with people you have nothing in common with, eat mediocre food and listen to tedious reports and presentations in the forgettable conference rooms of a seedy airport hotel just like a real male chauvinist pig at a sales conference.

Why let men have all the fun? Break down the barriers of male-dominated society and enjoy your fair share of stress, savage office politics and redundancy fears. Why

let your husband buy you your own car when you can trade long, hard hours for one on loan? In a week-long festival of feminine liberation you can attend seminars on a wide range of exciting new activities such as Completing Tax Returns, Waiting For Cancelled Trains or Grovelling for Promotion. Take part in our Simulated Business Situation and discover the thrills of being promoted beyond your level of competence, replaced by a computer or having to explain falling sales.

Female Chauvinist Sows

There's plenty of scope for enlightened feminist relaxation too. Our all-female courtesy-bus crews will take you on all-included trips to colourful building sites where you can whistle at brawny labourers or gaze up the eye-catching trouserlegs of men on scaffolding. In the evenings you can be raucous in expensive restaurants, get drunk, and pinch the bottoms of slim Italian waiters.

Afterwards you can
- shout abuse at male strippers
- swagger into the disco
- ogle young men
- swap blue jokes at the bar

There's no doubt about it, Kook's Feminist Festival will open the doors to a whole new anti-chauvinist world. Become complete and fulfilled, take your place in the dole queues with your male counterparts with pride. Our sports programme gives you the chance to discover the joys of boxing, rugby and tossing the caber, while our feminist beauty salon will transplant hair from your head to your entire body, remove those inhibiting role-dictating curves and increase your muscle mass.

Just imagine the pleasure of pouring our of the station after a day's work with all the other commuters, listening to your husband's tales of domestic disaster as you change plugs, mow the lawn or relax with a bit of car washing. Reverse roles right away with Kook's.

Disaster Movie Special

For those among us who relish the thrill of danger as an escape from the daily round, it gets harder and harder to find holidays that offer new challenges, new excitement. This is particularly true for those who crave a sense of adventure but don't want to subject their bodies to the gruelling physical demands of the conventional adventure holiday.

We at Kook's Tours have turned our attention to this problem and have come up with a heartstopping package designed to get the blood moving in even the most hardened adventurer. We like to think that **a Kook's Tour Goes where the Adrenalin Flows!** Our Disaster Movie Special is guaranteed to make hearts pound for you, your family and your insurance company.

The excitement begins the moment your ticket arrives when you discover that the actual cost is nearly ten times what you were led to expect, and that payment has already been made by Direct Debit from your bank account. Then it's all aboard the coach for the start of your vacation, and the first fun event.

Gasp with horror as the speeding coach goes out of control and slides over the edge of a precipice.

Cling desperately to strangers as it teeters precariously at the exact point of balance, then gaily hurl your luggage out of the windows to lighten the load. Once aboard our specially prepared airliner you can watch the ground fall away beneath you with a delicious sense of foreboding.

Bite your lip as the huge aircraft plummets and rolls to avoid some unseen object.

Giggle hysterically as the oxygen masks drop out of the ceiling and you discover that yours hasn't worked. There is no better way to meet new people than trying to tear off your neighbour's mask for that precious life-giving gas.

All too soon the thrill-packed flight is over and you are all in ambulances speeding towards your South Seas hotel in a desperate bid to outrun the yawning crevices opening up behind you on this earthquake-wracked island.

- Will you make it?
- Will the hotel still exist?
- Will you ever see your loved ones again?

We have no idea, which is what makes our Disaster Special such good value.

The hotel itself will be the latest thing in modern architectural technology. Nod appreciatively as the smooth high-speed elevators whisk you up to your rooms on the fortieth floor. And marvel at the superb view from your balcony. Sip exotic cocktails on the balcony as you observe the approach of a tropical hurricane heading straight for your little island paradise.

At night, the smell of smoke hardly disturbs your enjoyment of the soft, balmy evenings until it's too

Be the sole survivors of a mighty shipwreck and get to know someone better on a romantic fully-furnished island . . .

. . . or jog blithely through a picturesque jungle with the biggest toad ever breathing foul vapours down your neck. Then scramble screaming from its gaping jaws when you trip over a tough liana.

late. Then it's time for a bit of rushing round naked in the corridors looking for the non-existent stairway before hurling yourself down forty floors into the sparkling azure pool fringed by gently waving palms. Imagine the relief when you realise that the pool is not boiling after all . . . that it is just the thrashing of frenzied piranhas.

If you are one of the lucky ones who complete this idyllic sojourn, there is the voyage home to look forward to. Find a whole new perspective on life as the ship turns upside down in shark infested waters, trapping you in an airbubble shared only with a Great White and a leaking nuclear reactor.

Remember, if life seems not worth living . . . it's time for Kook's.

REALLY GREAT ADVENTURES!

Yomping Through The War Zones

Walk into almost any pub in the land for a solitary drink and an elderly man will sidle up and start telling you about the war. In lurid detail he will describe its horrors and deprivations, but it was clearly the most rewarding period of his life. We at Kook's began to suspect that a giant public deception was being practised and decided to research the matter. Every member of the armed forces we interviewed had the same answer: War is Hell! Then why, we wondered, were they in no hurry to buy themselves out?

The reason was all too clear! War is not hell — **war is terrific fun,** and the last thing soldiers want is thousands of civilians pouring on to the battlefields of the world and spoiling their sport. With great difficulty Kook's Tours have made exclusive arrangements to allow you to share the thrills and excitement enjoyed by soldiers the world over. A limited number of 'war correspondent' tickets are now available for this season's international conflicts . . . so book early to avoid disappointment.

FREE Rape and Pillage

Tour the front lines of all the major world conflicts, subject to availability. Wear dashing camouflage kit and chew old cigars. Rush about in jeeps breaking all known traffic regulations, and even **drive through private houses in tanks!** Liberate whole towns and enjoy the thrill of knocking the tops off wine bottles and pouring them over your face as pretty girls hit you with flowers.

When you're not busy liberating, there is plenty of rushing about in mud with important messages to be done. Dodge real bullets, throw back fizzing grenades and enjoy the camaraderie of your fellow men-of-war. Yomp over inhospitable terrain. And fall out of helicopters shouting and pointing at things. Soon it's time for digging little holes in the ground with your free spade, and once your have settled into your den (ocean view extra) take time off to examine all the exciting gifts the quartermaster has hidden in your pack.

Bloody your Bayonet

Don't miss the thrill of the dawn attack as you fix your sharp bayonet and run out into the smoke and din. There's plenty of fresh air and exercise and the chance to make as much noise as you like by firing bullets (first 100 rounds FREE) as fast as you can. Break windows and doors and run about in other people's houses stealing folkloric curios without getting into trouble. And remember, everything is absolutely FREE so don't worry about losing anything when the time comes for the counter-attack and retreat.

Fun With Mortars

As soon as the enemy have had their turn you can relax informally and eat rations out of your own private mess kit before putting in a bit of time on the mortars. And if desert warfare is not your thing, try one of the exciting South American coups, or while away a long weekend fighting with urban guerrillas in a war-torn holiday resort.

There's no doubt about it, war can make a healthy and unforgettable change from the daily grind. And there's nothing like a few medals and war wounds for getting you a seat on the board when the holiday is over.

1st 100
ROUNDS OF
AMMO
FREE!

Ballast Cruises

How often have you dreamed of sailing sun-kissed and silvered seas on a carefree luxury cruise? Imagine yourself sipping cocktails against the backdrop of a magnificent tropical sunset, the cares and woes of everyday life streaming away in your wake as you voyage to exotic lands and balmy climes. Now at last Kook's Tours can make your dreams come true at a price you *can* afford.

Book a Ballast Cruise with us and you can relax in the bosom of the deep and still have money to burn on those fun nights ashore. From the moment you step on to the deck amid the colourful workaday hustle and bustle of a busy quayside you will enjoy a holiday with a difference.

Linger awhile and savour the quaint colloquialisms of the stevedores as they go about their business. Gag in the rich aroma of the majestic deep. Leap out of your socks as the foghorn announces your departure. As the shoreline fades from view and the ship buries its proud nose in the first of many Atlantic rollers, the fresh, spray-filled gale will rip the hair from your head and whet your appetite for the culinary delights that await you.

International Cuisine

Almost every day, the experienced gallery staff will plan and prepare the best menu circumstances permit and will personally lower it to your private dining area in the spacious aft hold. And as you steam towards your first port of call, there will be plenty of opportunity to participate in the fascinating routine of shipboard life.

Gaze for hours at the majestic rise and fall of the horizon or take photographs of the smoke from the funnel streaming away like a dark banner. Watch the merry porpoises cavort with joyful exuberance as you deposit your colourful lunch over the taffrail. Smile wanly as the jovial crew shriek with kindly laughter from the bridge. For children too, the ship offers a wide range of entertainments from scores of intriguing nooks and crannies amongst the exotic cargo of coal slack, fish oil and tractor parts to the old-world wonders of bilge and chain locker.

Rocking and Rolling Through the Night

At night you can dance among the soft pools of moonlight filtering down the ventilator shafts to the primeval beat of ancient turbines, before falling exhausted into your FREE HAMMOCK. But even fighting off rats and splicing steel hawsers

Even leaks are fun in Kook's engine rooms!

Step aboard for romance.

begins to pall without some change of pace.

There is little to compare with the excitement of entering a foreign port with its myriad novelties and diversions. Unloading and loading do take some time, it's true, but once you have finished making your own contribution to the web of international commerce there will be plenty of opportunity to take in the sights and sample the local nightlife. The fun-loving and helpful crew will delight in helping you spend your money and will steer you away from the usual tourist traps. Then it's back to the ship with your souvenirs, many of which can be treated by the ship's own doctor.

All too soon, the voyage will be over and you will put the last shovelful of coal into the boilers. As you wend your way from frontier to frontier, embassy to embassy on the homeward journey, you will carry a host of memories and tattoos to remind you of a once-in-a-lifetime holiday you will probably never submit to again.

See the ocean from eye level . . . or admire the fittings of your luxury cabin.

Vintage Air Travel

Travelling by air today has achieved standards of speed and efficiency undreamed of by the early pioneers of commercial flight. Modern manufacturers and airlines have conspired to make the passenger feel that air travel is no different from going by bus or train. Indeed, it is often necessary to look out of the window to see whether you are on the ground or in the air.

The romance of flight is the first casualty of this impersonal approach, and there is a growing yearning for the days when destinations were approximate and the pilots wore ankle-length coats, goggles and small moustaches. Recapture this golden age with our Grand Old Days of Aviation Excursions.

Take our ten day (approximate) Continental Tour and you will experience the unique thrill of stepping aboard **our own ex-Imperial Airways, ex-Afghanistan Airlines Handley Page HP42 Hannibal.** One of the first luxury passenger liners, it is totally original and unrestored with no new-fangled electronic aids to spoil the authenticity of your flight through time.

Biggles Goes West

Our crew is also 100% authentic. Lured from retirement by their nostalgia for those glorious early days, they are unspoiled by the impersonal bureaucratic rituals of fitness tests and refresher courses. Some concessions, of course, have been made in the interests of passenger safety; their hearing aids (new batteries every trip), contact lenses and pacemakers are right up to date, and the old silk parachute canopies have been replaced with nylon.

The thrills begin the moment the aircraft struggles off the runway and lurches towards the cloud layer to a romantic 400 ft. There is intense rivalry for the window seats whenever one of the noble old 475hp radial engines shakes itself to pieces in a spectacular display of its handcrafted inner workings. Listen with bated breath to the nostalgic sounds of parting stays and shredding fabric once so familiar to early travellers.

Surprise Landings

Hear again the distinctive coughing and spluttering which signals the time for a refuelling stop and join with the crew in emptying can after can of benzine into the tanks. Then airborne again and, at last, the moment you have been anticipating. Marvel at the silence when all those great engines stop at once and the captain appears to instruct you not to panic. Watch the wild and desolate terrain rush up at you in a powerful demonstration of gravity. Go instantly unconscious to the sound of shattering propellers and rending spars.

ALL ABSOLUTELY FREE!!

What can match the romance of those sing-songs round the signal fire or of taking your turn at driving off the packs of ravening wolves as you watch your broken leg go gangrenous. Take unforgettable photographs as it is finally amputated by the captain with a rusty penknife. Help with dismantling the old Hannibal and carving a new prop for the homemade monoplane that's your

only chance. Learn just how complex is the science of avionics as it plummets off the cliff into the river far below.

And if you think this is great . . . next year we go international with the fabulous Lockheed Constellation just rescued from an old barn in Dorset. So book now.

plus
Build your own Plane

Happy holidaymakers enjoy some of the facilities of bustling Kook's International Airport.

Sahara Orienteering Party

The hard yellow sun beats down on the tiled roofs and dusty streets of the picturesque small Arab village. It is market day and the stalls are piled high with genuine Jaffa oranges and secondhand Touaregs. Throngs of Arab women, wrapped from head to toe in black sheets, collide with each other in the bustling bazaars. Small, barefooted children scamper merrily in and out of the crowd buying and selling their older sisters in a sort of juvenile stock exchange.

The scent of ancient history, remarkably similar to camel dung, hangs heavy in the air as you accept the taxi driver's generous tip and step from his Cadillac in front of the Kook's Tours local office for the start of your desert adventure. From there it's straight to the central market place, where he will guide you through the ancient rituals of buying your camel.

Free Camel Rental

Learn to spot a nice plump hump, ask to see their teeth, learn how to remove their teeth from your elbow. Before concluding the transaction, ask to be taken for a ride and the dealer is almost certain to oblige. The deal concluded, your party assembles for the start of your journey into the romantic world of Beau Geste.

Luck of the Legion

Under the leadership of our celebrated Sahara guide, Mark Thatcher, the camel caravan sets off across the burning sands while you follow closely to make sure that its wheels don't get clogged with grit. And don't forget to make sure that the windows are open to allow the camels a good supply of air.

Experience searing heat, turn crispy golden brown under burnished copper sun.

Dive headlong into mirages like real legionnaires.

In every direction, the boundless reaches of the desert stretch to the horizon like a shimmering, frozen sea. In that relentless heat, the chill of fear you feel when Mark asks you the way is a welcome change of temperature. Laugh at his silly mistake when you realise that his map is of the Gobi desert.

Be amazed at the nutritional value of leather shoes when the food runs out, and learn how to make the last last. It's interesting to note how much faster you travel on bare tippy-toes across the burning sands. Then just as you feel the strength

ebbing from your parched body a movement beind a ridge catches your eye. Magnificent in their tribal costumes, a prince of the desert and his noble band raise their arms to you in the time-honoured salute of one desert dweller to another.

With cries of welcome and a charming natural courtesy they gallop towards you, relieve you of the burden of your wallets and thunder into the heat haze. Experience real despair until the tousled heads of distant palms and ancient crenellated parapets point the way to salvation. A Holiday Inn! At last a cold shower and steaming platefuls of sheep's eyes and Turkish Delight to provide a festive end to a memorable adventure among the dunes of the Sahara.

Our celebrity guide scans the horizon.

Kook's camels are afforded every comfort.

Soccer Fan Orgy

Pounce on small policemen in the comfort of your own compound.

VILLA B

ample opportunity to run about at busy intersections and relieve yourself in public.

Crossings on the ferry have all been booked to ensure plenty of family groups, parties of nuns etc. among the other passengers to add to the pleasure of running amok in a confined space. What better way to have fun and meet lots of like-minded people than slithering in the bilges with fellow fans, or throwing darts down those funny great trumpet things sticking up from the deck.

Then the high point of the holiday really begins as the gangway leads you into a soccer fan's paradise. Rampage through street after street of greasy foreigners and laugh uproariously as they babble and wave their arms whenever you bellow

Tired of spending cramped and uncomfortable hours on overcrowded terraces waiting for something to happen to break the monotony of the game? Fed up with being surrounded by half-wits interested only in watching people run backwards and forwards across a field? Here at Kook's Tours we know what football is really about.

From the moment you step into one of our customized Cruise-o-Boozer coaches you will know that this is going to be a really great season. From the synthetic concrete benches to the stifling odour of packed and sweaty bodies, everything has been carefully designed to keep your irritability at fever pitch. All the seats face the opening windows to afford each passenger ample opportunity to abuse, shout at or be sick on innocent pedestrians on the way to the ferry.

Put the Boot In

Kick our on-board vending machines for a constant supply of warm beer and cold hamburgers served together in a single container so you can keep one hand free for throwing things at all times. The coach will make frequent stops in towns and cities, so you will have

Relax with friends in the bar.

obscenities into the doorways of their funny little shops. Our guide will show you all the places where you can eat and drink without having to touch any of that foreign muck, then it's on to the stadium.

Gratuitous Violence Absolutely Free

Imagine the thrill of a packed ground humming with anticipation. Suddenly the whistle blows and it's time for the fun to begin without the distraction of a game to watch. Just you, your friends and generous stockpiles of cans, broken bottles and lumps of concrete. Our trained supervisors will goad you to such unimaginable heights of unreasoning rage that in no time at all you will be tearing up the seats and biting each other's heads with the best of them. Learn new skills while having a great time.

Just as you begin to feel that the best is over, the chainlink fences are lowered and the local constabulary pour into the stands. Spit on bewildered little policemen, scamper away from baton charges all the way back through town. Put dents inside their vans and make faces at their superior officers; then get really mad when they lock you in the cells. Bite all the paint off the bars in retaliation for their outrageous behaviour.

Very soon embassy officials will arrange your release in time for you to enjoy some noisy, mindless bravado before boarding the ferry for the return trip home. Savour the joy of drinking yourself into oblivion or beating yourself unconscious against other supporters' heads without a care in the world. Our fleet of forklift trucks and cattle wagons are there to see you safely home.

Join rowdy hooligans just like you then ride home in our custom-built Superkruisers.

KOOK'S MINDER

KOOK'S TOURS

SUPERKRUISER

Anatomical Adventure

Educational holidays can be great fun as well enlightening, and may even change your life or help you to increase your income. One of today's most fascinating worlds is that of medicine, and you and your family can learn and play the Kook's Tours way with our unique Anatomical Adventure.

Enroll in our two week crash course and reduce your medical bills as you explore the fascinating world within your own bodies. With each ticket comes, entirely FREE

- A smart white gown and mask
- A plastic apron printed in full colour with the Hippocratic Oath
- A personalized set of real tools.

Group Surgery!

Why not get together with a group of enthusiastic friends with serious medical problems and qualify for your own private operating theatre and ward? We will allow you a special rate payable in advance. Each ward is luxuriously fitted out with everything you will need for a really exciting and realistic holiday. Saline drips, curtain screens, enema tubes and an unlimited supply of dustbin liners (for all the bits you don't want to keep as souvenirs) are available without further charges. The theatres too are just like the actual thing with tables and big lights and a dispenser for gloves and neat little hats.

Our staff are always on hand to advise you should you find yourself in difficulties, and can even take over if you feel that you have been a bit too ambitious. Save up all those niggling ailments like tonsils, appendix problems, wisdom teeth or ingrowing toenails for an adventure-packed vacation. Let your children get to know you inside as well as out as they tackle those uncomfortable kidney stones that have been bothering you for months.

Discover what makes each other tick and look deep into your loved one's eyes with little torches. The human body is amazingly complex and offers endless possibilities for self-discovery. The more you learn, the more there is to learn and you will be astonished at how quickly the removal of a simple corn or bunion can lead to the amputation of a complete limb. Towards the end of the first week you could win one of a variety of handmade, fully washable articulated limbs in a range of exciting fade resistant colours by entering our **Amputation of the Week Competition**.

Mix 'n' Match

During the second week you will want to try some more ambitious

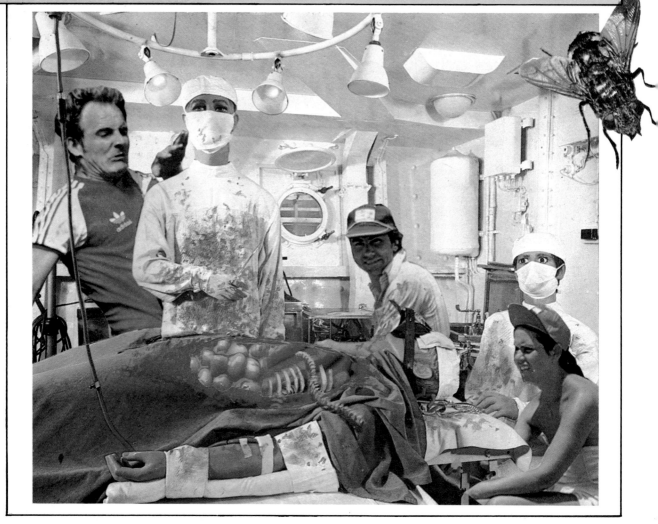

operations and may wish to participate in our group activities. These events allow you the opportunity to open yourself up to a new circle of friends. If you can find someone with cardiac problems, get straight to the heart of the matter and try a transplant or two in our well equipped Mix 'n' Match Theatre. Through mirrors and the miracles of modern anaesthetics you could perform your own pre-frontal lobotomy and ensure a life of relaxation and freedom from care by turning yourself into a vegetable.

Lastly, as a climax to your holiday you can participate in our exciting Frankenstein Finale. A brand-new, mains/battery electric wheelchair, fully taxed and insured, with steel-belted radials for superlative cornering and roadholding, is there to be won. It will be awarded to the team who can contruct the most lifelike homunculus from all the spare organs and limbs.

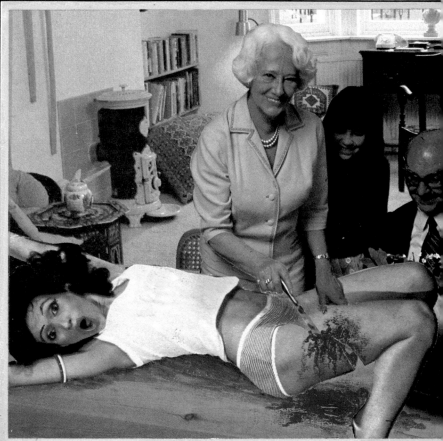

Have fun with friends, learn simple anaesthesia, or try a head transplant.

Sin Special

Why be content with the occasional night out with the boys, drinking a few beers, telling a few blue jokes and spending the rest of the night wandering seedy backstreets looking for where the action is? When you find it, you spend half the time worrying about how badly you'll be ripped off and the other half being uncomfortably aware of the huge gorilla lurking outside the door with a stopwatch and a small but deadly Italian knife.

FREE Pleasure Vouchers
Go the whole hog with Kook's on our Round-the-Clock Sin Special. Pack the indiscretions of a lifetime into a single fortnight. Specially recommended for novice monks who can get all their sins over with in one sitting (or lying down for the traditionalist). With each booking comes a Bumper Booklet of Pleasure Vouchers graded from a peck on the cheek to the truly unspeakable.

Happy Handful Hostesses
Our ex-Playboy executive jet is fully customized to provide every comfort as it speeds you to exciting venues from Albuquerque to Zanzibar where your every whim and fancy will be over-indulged. Between each bout of excess you can lounge in lascivious luxury at 25,000ft with our Happy Handful Hostesses and eat oysters and rhinoceros horns from the Libido Bar.

Visit the world-famous Texas Chicken Ranch and do fowl deeds. Get into bad habits with unfrocked nuns in Nantes. Use our special pass to enter a real harem with eunuchs on the door. Inside, a host of drug-crazed Turkish dancers vie for the chance of introducing you to the sensual mysteries of the forbidden east. Imitate temple wall carvings and adopt impossible positions in **Calcutta's fabled Kama Sutra Karnival Rooms.**

Electronic Orgies
When you think you have had s surfeit of pushing and shoving, try our Dial-an-Appliance service for the key to a vibrant new spectrum of experience.

Simply clip on a selection of our handcrafted attachments, plug yourself into the mains and go go go.

Wear tight rubber suits. Romp in vats of strawberry blancmange. Or hang from springs in our unique Sextravaganza Salon. Our blow-up doll dispenser operates on an exclusive credit card system so that you

only pay at the rate of inflation. Used in conjunction with the deluxe Masochists' Mattress bed of nails, you can feel confident that the orgy will go with a bang.

Swing All Night!

For the more jaded tastes we offer optional **Perversion Excursions** in colourful, aptly-named Bangkok. Grubby gaberdines and Polaroid camera supplied absolutely FREE! Frighten horses and elderly orientals with our steam operated mac flap-

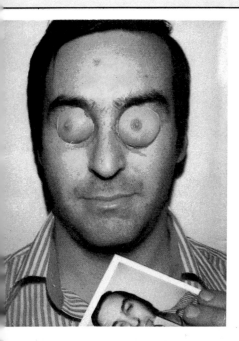

per. Or stuff your trousers with nettles and pineapples from the colourful local market. Try wearing our exclusive keyhole spectacles and feel deliciously guilty all day long. And if you like things the bigger the better and larger than life, then wallow in flesh at an

Outsize Orgy.

Swing all night to great organ music, swing from great organs all night! A great favourite!

As part of our introductory offer, the return fare is only half price because, as a shadow of your former self, you will be able to share a seat with one of your fellow holiday-makers. One of our couriers will accompany you to Passport Control to confirm that you are travelling on a younger man's passport, then it's into the ambulance and a quick vitamin supplement for the ride home.

- **Have Quite A Good Time**
- **Go All Over The Place**
- **Learn All About Reproduction**

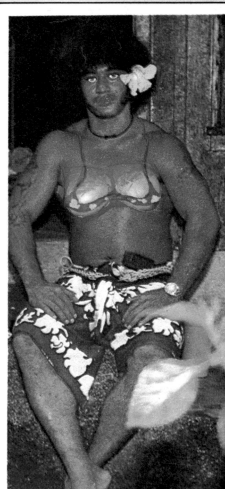

Boating Bonanza

The proud sloop bucked and shuddered in the fierce rip tide surging round the towering knee of rock. The fury of the current lashed the water to a creamy foam as she fought to outrun her sinister pursuer, but at last it was clear that the race was lost. There was nothing to do but stand and fight. She came about in the lee of a vast, smooth cliff and brought her guns to bear, rolling heavily in the swell as she waited. Seconds later an ominous shape nosed round the foam-flecked knee and the sloop heeled hard over under the recoil of her broadside. The sponge hit the water with a thunderous splash, a wall of water surged forward and a cheer rose from the brave sloop as the huge yellow duck capsized.

A Breeze In Your Rigging

Why be content to be a bathtub admiral when Kook's Boating Bonanza can put you at the tiller of a real boat? From pedalo to pinnace we have a holiday afloat to suit your experience. Even the absolute novice can take command of his vessel and feel the deck beneath his feet quiver with the surge of power as his family's feet turn the paddles into a blur. Explore the uncharted water of the boating lake. Come about and heave your mizzen into small brown paper bags.

Find some secluded anchorage and relax in the binnacle, the soft evening breeze humming in your trusses as you dream of distant

shores and munch your grog. Then it's time to set course for home, racing time and tide with only your capstan to guide you. At last you spy the welcoming beacon of a flashlight and hear the harbourmaster's timeless call . . . 'Come in number 3, your time is up'.

Hello Sailor

Learn the correct way to carry parrots, batten down your breeches for a heavy blow and answer the age-old call of the sea. A little basic knowledge and you could sail in convoy with others on a flotilla holiday under the experienced eye of a hoary old seadog whose barque is worse than his bight. Swing from the yardarm under clear Mediterranean skies, shiver timbers in romantic fishing ports or enjoy exotic foods with a clear sea forrard and a tender behind.

Steep yourself in brine and maritime lore. Learning knots, like not to do things into the wind and not to sit up suddenly in the night, is most important as they are used for everything from shanking sheep to measuring your speed, but do not confuse a rolling hitch with a rolling gait or you will take hours to unravel. Shipboard discipline too is very important, so as master of your craft

you will need to know about whipping ropes and beating to windward.

Kanal Kapers

If you prefer your water flat rather than corrugated, why not explore the charm of inland waterways on a Kook's Kanal Kaper? Leave the quay behind and barge through locks that haven't been changed for hundreds of years. Listen to the whispering of the breeze through the TV aerial and the soft gurgle of limpid waters around your cosy bunk as the narrowboat settles for the night. Savour the peace of unspoilt countryside as the family tow you through mile after mile of rural scenery.

Canoeing holidays are also popular as an aquatic camping vacation. Discover the thrill of unexpected weirs or look at fish very closely. Be amazed at how long you can hang upside down in locks before people notice that you are not a floating log. For a boating holiday that's worth its weight in flotsam, go overboard with Kook's.

Just a few choices . . . paddle the Zambezi with Max the parrot . . . cruise the Atlantic in an ocean-going pedalo . . . or linger in exotic harbours.

Trans-Siberian Steam Rally

The crimson glow from the firebox spills like liquid gold as another shovelful of coal is heaved into the furnace. Polished brass and copper gleam in the fierce firelight, then the angry roaring is suddenly silenced by the slamming of the cast-iron door. Dials and gauges respond to the fury within, and here and there stray wisps of steam escape from the maze of conduits and pipes. Sooty, sweaty hands deftly twirl stopcocks and vents to control the flow of power. There's a magic in old central heating systems that evokes a poignant nostalgia.

Steam railway engines have much the same effect. Who can recall those glorious monarchs of the railways without sensing that in the relentless march of progress, something magnificent has been lost. Here and there enthusiasts have managed to preserve something of this Golden Age, but for the visitor it is difficult to experience the full flavour of the pioneering days.

With the Kook's Tours Trans-Siberian Steam Rally you can rediscover the full glory of the age of steam.

- Step back in time
- Play a part in history
- Book a place on the Trans-Siberian Special Express

There are plenty of opportunities for basking in the lazy Siberian sunshine at trackside halts while your friendly couriers take their teabreaks.

From the moment you are loaded into one of its nostalgic cattle trucks with a fascinating cross-section of dissidents and social outcasts you will know that this is a holiday with a difference. Sniff the romance of steam as it filters warmly up through the floorboards and peer through quaint chinks as the great engine pounds through the night.

You will have the chance to take your place on the footplate with the engineers, helping to throw defectors into the firebox. Catch moths in your teeth as you lean out of the cab to watch the pounding pistons.

And leap headfirst into snowbanks to extinguish the romantic sparks from the funnel that have set your hair ablaze. The soft clacking of the wheels on the track will lull you to sleep, your feet scarcely touching the ground in the warm press of fellow enthusiasts.

Never a Dull Moment

Once at the railhead you can actually participate in the construction of the track, just like those rugged pioneers of yesteryear. Imagine the thrill of hewing a path through solid rock, spanning deep gorges and bridging the wild fury of snow-swollen rivers with your bare hands! And at night you can sit back and enjoy the traditional camaraderie of labour camps the world over.

But the glory of the steam age is not just the trains and the monumental feats of engineering. It also lies in the small day-to-day activities of running a railway. Share absolutely FREE with generations of dedicated railmen the pleasures of greasing points and signal wires, stacking and loading coal, filling paraffin lamps and polishing acres of smoke-stained metal. Mingled with these joyous and satisfying tasks is the business of staying alive in inhospitable environments.

When at last the holiday is over, and you are packed into the trucks for the long ride home, you can savour the knowledge that you have experienced the magic of the railways as few people have. A real railman now, you can contemplate your frostbite and spreading gangrene with the pride of a dying breed.

Fresh home cooking all the way . . . and the chance to learn how to catch and skin dingoes and wombats with your bare hands.

Costa Packet Spenderama

- Cash in your investments
- Surrender your insurance policies
- Pawn your valuables
- Mortgage your house

then spend, spend, spend on the holiday of a lifetime with Kook's Tours. Never again will you have to endure the holiday reminiscences of your friends. And let's face it . . . the only reason you take a vacation at all is to keep pace with your social set.

Just think — with **one incredible spree** you can put an end to the tedious annual ritual of crowded airports, beaches and hotels. And surly foreigners. And silly local dishes. Put yourself on the very pinnacle of the social ladder. True, the cost is truly amazing, but it will be more than recouped by the savings of staying at home for the rest of your life.

Meet the Aristocracy!
But what will you get for your money? Prestige, and plenty of it! You will start to enjoy the benefits

two weeks before the vacation even begins, when we send you a selection of personal invitations from some of the impoverished but socially impressive European aristocrats on our books. Displayed in your home, they will be the envy of all your friends. Each one comes embossed with an authentic crest and includes a brief but warmly familiar personal note from the aristocrat concerned, absolutely FREE!

Red Carpet All the Way!
Then on the Sunday morning of departure, while your neighbours are all grubbing about in their gardens or washing the car, a Rolls Royce will arrive to collect your baggage. Shortly afterwards the helicopter will descend to take you to the airport. The red carpet is unrolled and you board, pursued by our reporters and photographers. Full pages are taken in the newspapers of your choice to cover the event.

Personalized Concorde!
At the airport the specially chartered Concorde awaits, resplendent in

your own top French Chef and a host of fairly famous people to feed you grapes etc. **all at your own, personal expense.** No opportunity for you to spend money like water will be overlooked and our helpful and

obsequious staff will do all they can to help you exceed yourself.

When at last the time to leave has arrived, and your stay has gone, your fur-lined Concorde will whisk you back home. Once there, a massed band of pipers from the Queen's Own Highlanders will escort you to a 21-gun salute and dinner with the Royal Family.

By the time you are back at your own front door, listening to the fading sirens of your motorcycle escort and shaking the last wisps of ticker-tape, we guarantee you will have enjoyed a unique vacation, or a bit of your money back.

new paintwork bearing your name. Inside, the jacuzzi, sauna and massage parlour will help to while away the minutes to St Moritz, where you will spend two exciting days lounging around on your specially reserved slopes in our FREE Pierre Cardin skiwear.

Then it's off for a romantic interlude in your private suite in the famous Taj Mahal. Waterski on the ornamental lake; throw our complimentary money at ethnic poor people, then explore the exotic bazaars of the East as our guests. When the thrill of buying everything in sight with your very own money has worn off, you will be able to enjoy the quiet elegance of the QE2 on the way to Hawaii.

Waiting for you there will be a First Class hotel booked entirely for you,

Amaze your neighbours as you arrive home in a royal coach (optional extra) or be the first ever to waterski round India's fabled Taj Mahal (takeaway service available).

Old Macdonald's Health Farm

Feeling tired and listless? Is your hair dry, lifeless and unmanageable? Are you prone to unsightly blemishes or just plain obese? Why pay huge fees and be pestered by expensive consultants when you could be a guest of one of the most revolutionary figures in the health and beauty industry.

By exclusive arrangement with Mr Macdonald, Kook's Tours can offer you the chance of a place in his unique, ideally situated establishment. Benefit from his lifetime's experience of modern farming methods and lose pounds (or any other negotiable currency). Only the most up-to-date techniques are employed, often using equipment adapted by old Macdonald himself, with the help of EEC subsidies, to deal with even the most intimate problems.

It's Biological

For the overweight, the strictly controlled diet of straw and water produces breathtaking results. Drawn from the farm's own old-world-style pond, the rich, nutritious variety of microscopic organisms and scientifically recognized liver flukes will have that hideous flab off you in no time. Extreme cases are dealt with by old Macdonald himself. With a snip snip here and a snip snip there clients are transformed, and an experienced seamstress is on hand to elegantly retailor all that spare skin. A few tucks and pleats and you could **be the centre of attention at any nudist gathering**.

Treatment is also available for the painfully thin under the supervision of the renowned Mr Gummidge. Now you can be the shape you always longed for. Astonish your friends and family, intrigue small childen, and frighten birds. Traditional techniques employed allow you to alter your size and shape whenever you choose and enormous savings can be made in the cost of your wardrobe. Clients are, however, advised not to stand too close to open fires.

And don't miss the unique beauty treatments at old Macdonald's Health Farm. From head to toe, you can be transformed from a wrinkled, scabrous harridan into something unforgettably different. Hair-weaving specialists use the

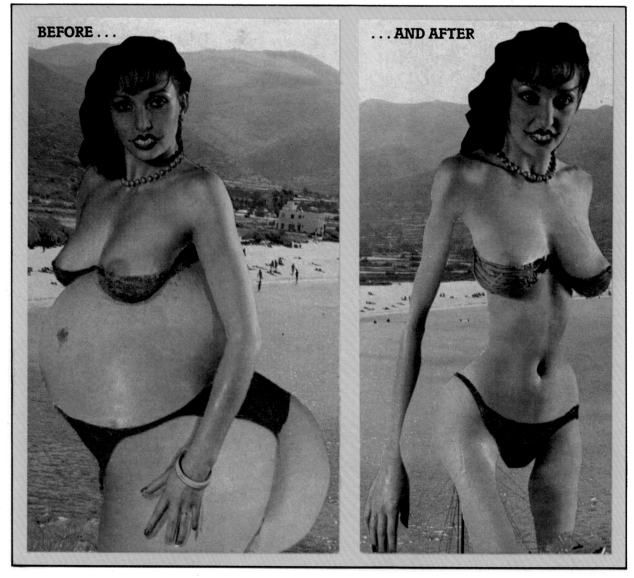

BEFORE ...   ... AND AFTER

latest in fade-resistant, highly durable polyethylene baling twine in self-impregnated colours ranging from orange to red to restore your head's crowning glory. Guaranteed tangle free, each strand is matted into place by hand.

Skin care too is important. Wrinkled or pitted skin is smoothed over with layer after layer of hand-trowelled filler and ethnic putty, then sanded down to a perfect finish using only the finest grades of wet-and-dry. A top coat of clear polyurethane varnish gives good weather protection as well as a deep, lasting shine that will be the envy of your friends.

Cosmetic surgery is usually only available to a wealthy few, but at Macdonald's Health Farm it is offered entirely FREE for an introductory period only. **Have your least attractive features remodelled. Or have them removed entirely.** Choose from a huge selection of some of the world's most beautiful bits or, for those on a limited budget, from a large Sheraton-style box of pre-owned features donated by previous clients. Even your closest friends will fail to recognise you when you return home!

Whatever your problem old Macdonald has the answer. Even the ugliest client can be cured in a good smokehouse.

Just look what Old Macdonald's can do for you!

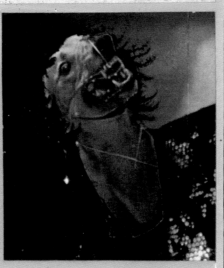

Kiddy Kamps The Woodshed Way

Taking children on holiday means no holiday for you! Keeping them amused in a strange country for two weeks will push you slowly towards madness and bankruptcy and there are times when you will want to bury them up to their necks in the sand while you rush off, get magnificently drunk and commit indiscretions with sinewy foreigners in the local disco.

Kook's Kiddy Kamps are just what you have been dreaming of! While you jet off to the sun, your children can enjoy their own exciting vacation in our care. We undertake to feed and entertain them, and we will turn them into model young-

sters under the expert supervision of our own unique Barbarella Woodshed.

Well known for her uncanny ability to communicate with children in their own language, Barbarella's training techniques will get the very best from your offspring.

> *We didn't recognise them when we collected them'* – The Kings of Herts.
>
> *'I've never seen Jimmy's nose so wet'* – Mrs. Asgood-Azamile.

Discipline and affection are Miss Woodshed's watchwords. From the moment they arrive, children lose

no time in getting into the swim of things. They are thrown straight into the olde-worlde sheepdip. 'Children should be clean enough to eat off', barks the lovable Barbarella. Her warmth and cheerful manner are much appreciated by her young charges. Whenever she arrives at the compound they run about with tremendous enthusiasm, digging holes, building vaulting horses and trying to leap over the chainlink fencing in an endearing attempt to gain her attention.

Nourishing Marrowbone Jelly

Physical health and mental alertness are the order of the day as Miss Woodshed puts the children through their paces on the assault course. Vaulting walls, crawling through drains and under barbed wire do wonders for healthy appetites and the children learn to look forward to feeding time. Only choice cuts of lean meat enriched with vitamins and bone meal and thoroughly recommended by top breeders are used.

Obedience Training

There are classes in walking to heel, sitting on command and good posture for those parents who hope to show their children. Our stick-throwing machine is always a great favourite with the younger ones. The older child keen to learn new skills can choose from a variety of special classes such as helping the blind, sniffing out drug caches or herding sheep into pens.

Miss Woodshed is quite prepared to deal with any problems your child may have such as snapping at the wheels of moving cars or leg-clasping houseguests. 'There isn't a child alive who can't be cured of habits', growls affable Barbarella. 'The secret is to offer a sympathetic ear and a thrashing to within an inch of their little lives'. And with someone so in tune with the needs of youngsters, no wonder there are screams of delight every time she appears.

In the evenings the children are allowed to seek their own amusements or relax quietly in their kennels, while on rainy nights, as a special treat, they can curl up in front of the fire until walkies time. In Barbarella's own words, 'The quality of instruction here is so high that not a single child has ever returned'. What greater testimonial to Miss Woodshed's ability can there be?

Children can participate in a wide range of outdoor activities.

Healthy young appetites are well catered for in our modern and hygienic kitchens.

No Sex At All!

Your kiddies can be sure of a warm welcome from our own Barbarella Woodshed. Private tuition and discipline can be arranged.

KOOK'S TOURS
Funseeker Booking Form

SPECIAL OFFER: BUY JUST 23 HOLIDAYS AND GET ONE **FREE**

Your chosen holiday	
Number of people – dead or alive, (amputees 10% discount)	

Type of Accommodation	Surcharge
Open Air	No Charge
Bunkhouse	£1.00 per nite
Private Quarters	£5.00 per nite
Straw-filled Box	Exercise wheel extra

Facilities Required	
Bath	£1.00
Ditto, with taps	£5.00
Ditto, with taps & water	£20.00
Ditto, with plug	Not Available
Own toilet	Carriage extra
One of ours	£10
Ditto with Kook's Supaflush	Handles optional but advisable
Sheets	Perforated – £5 extra
Connecting Rooms	If you don't have connections, how did you get hold of this brochure?

Board	
No Board	£5.00
Very Board	Free
Half a Board	£3.00
A Whole Board	£4.00

Diet	
Yes or No	
Kosher	Not Available
Vegetarian	Not Available
Bread & Water	No charge
Crunchy Mollusc Fibre Diet	20p per day

Preferred Departure Airport	
Kook's International	£25 airport tax plus £25 parking or we dismantle your car

Preferred Departure Date

☐	February 30th	No Charge
☐	June 31st	No such date
☐	July 1st	£50 per head – rest of body FREE

Deferred Departure date

☐	Later, later	All monies in advance

Duration of Holiday

☐	7 days (2 nites)	See price list
☐	14 daze (3 nites)	Pull curtains for extra nites
☐	Life	Save £50 on one-way tickets

Travel Class Required

☐	Hold	No charge
☐	Steerage	2p per mile
☐	Form 4a	2 O'Levels
☐	Tourist	50p per gallon
☐	Livestock	1 gallon per p.

Groups, preferred companions

Age		☐	Under 25
		☐	25
Sex		☐	Either
		☐	Both
		☐	Yes (by negotiation)

Number of Children in Party
Will you require any other meals?

Your Name:

Address:
Postcode:

Remittance enclosed £   ,000.43p

(Tickets and confirmations will be sent to your address IMMEDIATELY after your departure)

Small print

Notwithstanding any written or other statement hereinelsewhere or hereinafter contained, any offer made herein by Kook's Tours (hereinafter called the Company) shall not expressly be deemed to be an offer unless specifically expressed as a bonafide offer in writing by an appointed officer of the company and specifically and correctly addressed to an individual (hereinafter known as the Victim) whereby it is agreed between the Company and the Victim or his successors and assigns as the case may be that should either party and particularly the Company go into receivership or liquidation other than a voluntary liquidation for the purposes of reconstruction the Company shall have the free and unencumbered right without giving notice of such to the Victim to sequester all sums of money whether in used or new notes, cheques, postal orders, Irish coins and the like previously remitted by the Victim to the Company and the Victim shall have no constraint on such action by the Company and the Company shall have no responsibility legal financial moral or humane to the Victim whatsoever and shall have no obligation legal financial moral or humane to supply any of the services activities or events described or offered in its literature notwithstanding howsoever such descriptions or offers are expressed and the Victim enters into this contract which shall be binding on the Victim but not the Company of his or her own free will for the duration of his or her natural or unnatural life and serve him or her right for not bothering to read all this whereby I do now set my seal signed Stewart Cowley ® trademark of Invisible Enterprises Ltd. somewhere in the Pacific.

Your Complaints

POST TO:

Name

Address